He Saw the Best in Me:
A Story of New Identity

He Saw the Best in Me: A Story of New Identity

KEDEISH SUKHDEO

StoryTerrace

Text Mollie Nelson, on behalf of StoryTerrace
Design Grade Design and Adeline Media
Copyright © Kedeish Sukhdeo
Text is private and confidential

First print March 2020

StoryTerrace

www.StoryTerrace.com

CONTENTS

1. A PAINFUL BEGINNING — 7
2. MY ESCAPE AND MORE FAMILY TROUBLES — 31
3. A NEW LIFE AND OLD TROUBLES — 37
4. DARKER DAYS — 43
5. NEW BLESSINGS AND BEGINNINGS — 51
6. GOD CAN TAKE ANYBODY FROM LOW TO HIGH — 57

1

A PAINFUL BEGINNING

My name is Kedeish Sukhdeo. I'm a victim of molestation and was abused by family members throughout my life. I've been mistreated, brought low, and rejected—but I survived, thanks to God. This is my story.

I was born and grew up in Lakes Spend District, Spanish Town P.O., Jamaica, in the West Indies. My mother, Norma Maxine James, was sixteen years old when she gave birth to me. My father, David A. Rowe, was her schoolteacher. He got her pregnant when she was very young and she had my older brother when she was fourteen. My mother's family were Christians, led by my great-grandmother who founded a church. She was a very spiritual woman and guided my mother's family with wisdom but the family started to fall apart after she passed away. I originally lived with my mother and her mother as a child. We were happy until the death of my younger brother. That was when everything fell apart.

When my mother was eighteen, my father got her pregnant with my younger brother, Blacker. However, when he was born he died from a sickness. After his death, my parents' relationship ended.

That was when my grandmother, my father's mother, started to manipulate him. She told him to take me and my brother away from my mother. She did it because she wanted the child support money that my father would have otherwise given to my mother. She hated my mother. His whole family did. They wanted to hurt her and didn't care if they hurt me and my brother in the process.

At the age of nine, in 1989, I was taken away from my mother, my brother, and everything I had known to live with my father's family. He'd been fighting her for a while, and every time he tried to take my older brother, my brother had resisted by hiding or running away. But I was too young to know what to do. I can remember crying every day and begging God to bring my mother back to me. No one in my father's family would let her come see me and she eventually moved away for work.

In my grandmother's house, I had no protection. My grandmother had always controlled my father and made him care for her children. He was a better father to her children than he was to his own. He never showed me love. That lack of love from my father and his family left me exposed, and soon I became a victim of molestation.

I was molested by four different family members: my step-grandfather, two uncles, and the father of my two younger brothers. I was ten the first time it happened.

My grandmother lived in a three-bedroom house and many of her family members lived with her, so there wasn't much room to go around. One night, my grandmother and auntie had gone to a party, and I was sleeping in my grandmother's and step-grandfather's room. I remember slowly waking to the sensation of my step-grandfather doing things to me with his mouth and his penis. I didn't know what to do, so I just lay there, afraid to move or say anything. When my grandmother and auntie returned from the party, my auntie peeked through a hole in the door to check on me and saw what my grandfather was doing. She coughed loudly to let him know that someone knew about what was happening, and he stopped. But no one said anything about it after that.

Soon after that, my grandmother moved me into the room where my two high school-aged uncles slept. One night, one of my uncles went to a party and everyone else was gone except for me and my other uncle. I remember waking up to find my panties had been taken off and were covered in slime. It was like what had happened with my step-grandfather so I knew that my uncle was molesting me, too. Another time, my first uncle was gone and the second one was home. It took me longer to fall asleep that night because I was afraid something bad was going to happen but I couldn't keep my eyes open for long. Soon, I fell asleep and woke to my uncle doing inappropriate things to me. I was slimy and wet again.

This happened multiple times, with both of my uncles, and my family did nothing. I would walk around in my slimy, bloody clothes, hoping they would see the evidence of what had happened to me. If they did, they said nothing. In the place where I grew up, if a young girl was molested, she had to keep silent about it. If she didn't, she would either be killed or left in the bushes to die.

My family liked keeping secrets and they punished me to make sure I kept what was happening a secret. The molestation went on for a few years and they never listened to me. I prayed to God for relief, and although He helped me by leading my aunt to discover what my step-grandfather was doing, it would be a few years before He would help me escape my grandmother's house.

My grandmother's family would punish and neglect me. They denied me food and feminine hygiene products. One time my cousin burned the clothes that my mother had sent to me as revenge for me telling my grandmother that he was looking at a pornographic magazine. I knew a lot of the punishment happened because my grandmother's family hated my mother, and hated me because I looked like my mother, but I also knew it happened to keep me from telling my father that I was being molested.

I didn't receive any protection from my grandmother or other members of her family. I was forced to sleep in the same beds as the men who molested me and was in turn blamed for being molested. My father didn't know about what was happening for about a year. The family didn't want to ruin his reputation or distract him from his work. When they did tell him, they lied and said I had wanted to have sex with these men. Nothing could be further from the truth. How can a young girl, from ages ten to twelve, give sexual consent to an adult man? I didn't even know how to care for myself, much less how sexual relationships worked. It was so sad. It's something that still hurts to think about.

Eventually, the abuse and neglect that I was subjected to began to influence my education. I had a dream as a child that I wanted to become a professional runner, a track star. I participated in races at school but soon enough my performance at school began to suffer

HE SAW THE BEST IN ME

in many ways because of what I was going through at home. I prayed to God throughout those years, and finally, when the timing was right, He helped me escape.

Me and my brother, Steven. I was two years old and Steven was four years old; we are two years apart.

Our second son, Ronaldo's, 21st birthday celebration, December 11

HE SAW THE BEST IN ME

Happy life, happy wife. Glory to God, you did it!

Mother's Day 2019: I was just feeling myself, beautiful as ever, Jesus' new creation

My husband with my second son, Ronaldo, my older daughter, Bianca, and my youngest daughter, Gabriella

My pastor, husband, best friend, and a wonderful father to our children. Family for life!

Mother's Day 2019: I was just giving God all the glory

HE SAW THE BEST IN ME

Me and my beautiful daughters at the movies: Princess Bianca and Princess Gabriella (I give thanks to God)

My firstborn son, Mr. J. Wallace

My two sons that God blessed me with; I love them so much.
Thank you, Jesus, for such a wonderful blessing.

HE SAW THE BEST IN ME

Me and my husband, Mr. and Mrs. Sukhdeo, during our five-year anniversary celebration in South Beach, Miami (2019)

My best friend and also my husband. Thank God for this wonderful man of God! He is a true example of a godly man.

HE SAW THE BEST IN ME

Me and my brother, Steven, at my sixth grade graduation from Whichport Primary School, age twelve

HE SAW THE BEST IN ME

Our firstborn son, Mr. J. Wallace, deployed to Korea (2019)

HE SAW THE BEST IN ME

Me and my husband, Thakur, just in traditional attire attending a friend's wedding

Me and my husband, Thakur; I was just showing him how beautiful the sky is

Friends, family, and even my parents gave up on me but God didn't give up. I thank God for every blessing He brought to my life: my beautiful children and wonderful husband. He saw the best in me and gave me a new life, glory to God.

Celebrating New Year's Day, 2019, with my husband, our beautiful son, Giovanni Ronaldo, daughters, Bianca and Gabriella, and also my daughter-in-law, Natalya

Jesus saw the best in me and gave me a new identity. I give God all the glory.

Just having a romantic moment on our five-year anniversary celebration

2
MY ESCAPE AND MORE FAMILY TROUBLES

When I was twelve years old, some relatives, from my mother's side of the family who went to school with me, told me that my mother had come back from working in Curacao. She had moved there two years before to find a job to support me and my brothers. No one, not even the fathers of her children, was giving her financial support. She had to provide for her family on her own.

I didn't wait until school was finished. I just took my things and ran back to Lakes Pen to see my mother again. After we reunited, I told her about everything that had happened to me in my grandmother's house. She cried and told me that it was going to be okay, and no one would ever hurt me again. She said I'd never have to go back to my father or his family.

The next day, my father came looking for me. My mother told him to go and said that if he didn't she would go to the police and tell them everything. She told him that his whole family would end up in jail for what they had done to me. My father didn't want to deal with the embarrassment of having his family's mistreatment of me made public, so he left me with my mother.

After that, I lived with my mother, three brothers, and my maternal grandmother. We lived in a house that had a big yard that was attached to three other houses. I helped to care for my brothers and our home when my mother went back to Curacao to look for another job. During that time, I felt strengthened in my faith. I felt that God had heard me and answered my prayer. Everything was going well: I was with my mother's Christian family and was going to church regularly. My life was better. And then we stopped hearing from my mother.

My mother's family started to say bad things about her after her communication stopped. This was around the time when they were falling apart after my great-grandmother's death, so my mother's absence gave them an opening to hurt her. They would tell me terrible things about her. They would say that she was working as a prostitute in Curacao. They also told lies to other people outside of the family.

Because my mother had moved away, and her family had started telling lies about her, life became hard again. My mother's family neglected me and my brothers. I had to steal underwear and pads from one of my cousins just to take care of myself. I tried to ask my father for help since my mother's family would do nothing to aid me and my brothers but he turned us away. I prayed hard for God to send someone who could show me the love I was missing from my life. Around that time, I met the man who would become the father of my first child.

HE SAW THE BEST IN ME

He was about twenty years old when we met. He was also married, but said he was separated from his wife. I viewed him as a friend at first, since he offered to help me and my brothers financially and seemed to genuinely care about us. I wasn't interested in anything besides his friendship because he was married, but that didn't matter to him. One day, he asked me to meet him after school for lunch in Port Henderson Beach, which was where he worked. After the lunch was over, he took me to a private hotel room and forced me to have sex with him. This became a weekly habit, and in 1995, I found out I was pregnant with my first child. I was fifteen years old.

I still didn't want to have a relationship with this man. I enjoyed the loving aspect of my relationship with him but hated the sex. I also wanted to go back to school to become a track star. I told him everything and at first he denied my baby was his child, even though he was the only man I was seeing at that time. He said he wouldn't divorce his wife because she was pregnant with their second child. I wouldn't have even been in a relationship with him had I known all this. I was young and didn't know better.

A few months after I broke off my relationship with this man, my mother finally returned. The reason she hadn't contacted me or my brothers was because she had been extremely sick. I told her about what had happened with the man I'd been in a relationship with and my pregnancy, and she was heartbroken. I'm her only daughter and she wanted only the best for me. She promised to take care of me and my baby and she kept every promise she made.

HE SAW THE BEST IN ME

When my son was born, his father returned. He wanted both me and his son back. He had two daughters with his wife and wanted a son. But I told him no and said that he should stay with his wife. I only asked that he support his son. My mother also told him to leave us alone. However, he would not listen. For a month, the father of my child would show up at my house and abuse me as punishment for refusing to give up my son and live with him. But after a month, I finally found help.

My cousin's half-brother, who had moved in with my family, helped fight off my child's father one day when he came to my house. He didn't come back after that. I started to cook for my cousin's half-brother, and it wasn't very long before we developed feelings for each other. He was the first man I ever had genuine feelings for.

Around the same time, a bad man started to pay attention to me. He was the sort of man that you couldn't just tell to go away. He was dangerous. My mother learned of this and started working on a way to get me out of Jamaica.

At the same time, my relationship with my cousin's half-brother continued to progress. We didn't want to act on our feelings for each other because we were technically family, but we couldn't help ourselves. We slept together twice, and after the second time, I became pregnant with my second child. He became suspicious and asked me if I was pregnant, but I told him that I wasn't. After that, I began to hate my cousin's half-brother. I enjoyed the emotional aspect of our relationship, but I hated the sex. I was still hurting from my father's family molesting me.

HE SAW THE BEST IN ME

My mother had finished her plan to get me away from where I was living, so I went to live with her in Curacao. Shortly after I moved in with my mother, a man named Raymond Martinez began to court me. He didn't know I was pregnant at first, but when I told him, he said he wanted to take care of me and be a father to my child. My mother didn't approve of Raymond because she didn't like his family, and I realized I wanted something different for Raymond. I liked him a lot, but I felt that he should be with a different person.

One day, I found out that my grandfather was getting papers for me to move to the United States. I was excited! Life in Curacao wasn't very easy for me. I wasn't born there, so I couldn't work there. I would have to return to Jamaica and leave my eleven-month-old son with my mother, but I wanted to support myself and my children. The opportunity to move to the United States felt like a chance at a new life.

3

A NEW LIFE AND OLD TROUBLES

I came to the United States on January 20, 2000. It was a bittersweet time for me because I was forced to leave my two sons behind in two different countries. My father, who had already moved to the United States, told me that he wanted to give me a new life without children. I didn't know at the time that I could have brought my sons with me since they were minors. It breaks my heart to think about it. I love both my sons so much, but I was young at the time and still naïve. I couldn't read or write very well, so I didn't know those things.

My father and brother already had jobs in the United States, and my father told me that I should go back to school and start working too. I got my first job at Universal Studios, and later got another job at a Cash and Carry grocery store. My father had insisted I get a second job.

It wasn't long before I learned my father's true motives for making me work so hard. He began to take advantage of me and my brother financially. He used my social security number, my name, and my credit score to take out large loans. He also took most of the money I received from my paychecks. Debt collectors started to call me and I didn't understand why. When I asked my father about it, he told me that it was my responsibility to pay back the loans he had taken out.

In August 2000, my father bought a house with the money he'd been taking from me and my brother, as well as with the loans he'd taken out in my name. After he bought the house, things only got worse. He continued to take more and more money from me to spend on himself and the house. I almost always had nothing to send to my children, and when I did have a little to send, he would tell me that I had to take care of the house for him. I realized then that my father wasn't going to be a real father to me. All I could see in front of me was a user and an abuser.

Around this time, a man who worked for Universal Studios' taxi service began to pressure me to be in a relationship with him. He had been providing me with transportation to my second job because I couldn't afford to take the bus every day. He said he was a Christian, but he was married. At first, he hadn't asked me for anything, but then he started asking me to be his girlfriend. I didn't want anything to do with a married man after the relationship I'd had with the father of my eldest son, but I didn't let him know that. Instead, I decided to use the situation to my advantage. It's not something that I'm proud of, but it helped me gain the little bit of financial independence I needed. One day, I told this man that my birthday was coming up, and that I wanted an expensive present. When I told him the amount of money I would need for this "present," he gave me that exact amount. After that, I didn't ride in his taxi. Instead, I used the money he'd given me for transportation and other needs.

I also began to make friends with my coworkers at Universal Studios. I became close with two people in particular: David, a white man, and Thomas, a black American man.

One day as we were both leaving work, I felt the urge to call out to David. I didn't know why I felt that way. I just had a feeling that I should say something to him. The following day, I felt very sick and didn't go in to work. When I returned the day after, I learned that David had died of a cocaine overdose while he was at a club. He had died the same day that I had felt the urge to call out to him. I was so sad and kept crying throughout the day at work.

After David's death, Thomas and I became closer. Thomas knew about my financial troubles and my father's abuse, so he invited me to live with him and his mother in the projects. It was good to be away from my father's house but living with Thomas had its own problems. He would invite his friends over and they would all smoke in the apartment. It wasn't a well-ventilated space. The apartment had one tiny window that couldn't open. I developed asthma from breathing in the smoke so often.

I also learned that Thomas had romantic feelings towards me. Although I didn't feel the same way about him, he respected me, which allowed us to maintain our friendship. I trusted him enough to fall asleep in his arms. But it wasn't long before a friend at work began to manipulate my relationship with Thomas. She would tell me that Thomas was a bad person and that I shouldn't be around him. Then she would tell Thomas lies about me. Her interference damaged our relationship so badly that it ended.

After my friendship with Thomas fell apart, I decided to sublet a room from a Jamaican man. I thought it would be a better situation, but it wasn't. He began to make inappropriate advances and violate my boundaries. One thing he would do was come into the bathroom to talk when I was taking a shower. I would tell him to leave, but he wouldn't listen. He finally kicked me out after I refused to be his girlfriend.

I moved into a house owned by two Canadian brothers. They seemed to be trustworthy people and I moved into the room they were subletting the same day I put down my deposit. Another man rented the only other available bedroom in the house, but after a few months, the brothers moved out and returned to Canada. The bank foreclosed on the house and I didn't know what to do. I stayed in that house for four months until the bank left a notice on my door telling me to vacate by February 2001. It gave me a little time but I still didn't know what to do. I had no money and nowhere to go.

That's when I reached out to my brother. I told him about what had happened and he encouraged me to reach out to our father to ask him if he would let me move back into his house. It took awhile for me to gather the courage to call him, but I did. My father said it would be okay for me to move back into the house and claimed that he wanted to restore our relationship. I believed him, but he was lying. He was in financial trouble again and said that he needed my help.

My father took all of my savings. I had been saving money for three months while I was renting from the brothers from Canada, but as soon as I returned to my father's house, he took everything I had. He had also moved his girlfriend and her grown children, one daughter and two sons, into the house. Even though we lived in close quarters with one another, I was once again ostracized and mistreated by my father's family. My father's girlfriend didn't like that one of her sons had to give up his room for me. She didn't want me there at all. Every day, she would go to my father with lies. She would tell him that I wasn't doing any cooking or cleaning and that her daughter was forced to do everything, even though I did a lot of the work. Her daughter would do her nails and sit on the computer all day. They were allowed to go into my father's bedroom, but I wasn't, even though I helped him buy the house. One day, I got into a fight with my father's girlfriend. She pulled a knife on me and said, "I will kill you and drink your blood." I knew then that I had to leave.

During this time, the only person who defended me was my father's girlfriend's nephew. He would tell my father that my father's girlfriend and her daughter were lying about me. He had feelings for me and asked me to move in with him, but I wasn't sure. It felt too soon. I didn't know if I loved him, and since I'd become a Christian in 1999, I decided that I wouldn't live with a man out of marriage.

I realized something when this man asked me to move in with him, and it was something that began to change how I viewed my life. I realized that every time I needed help, I always turned to a man as my escape.

4
DARKER DAYS

After my fight with my father's girlfriend, life started to become more complicated. I began to work two jobs again as a way to get my financial independence back. At the same time, my father's girlfriend's nephew began to show romantic interest in me. However, I wasn't sure if I wanted to begin a relationship with him. I was trying to live for God, but I also wanted to leave my father's house. The nephew told me that he could get me a place but only if I would live with him. I decided to start a relationship with him as a way to escape my situation, but I knew I didn't want to move in with a man I wasn't married to.

Thankfully, I didn't have to move in with him. Instead, I moved in with a coworker from a park I was working at, Wet 'n Wild. My coworker was a good woman and at first our living situation worked well—until she met my boyfriend. The moment she laid eyes on him she wanted him for herself and became very jealous. And because of her jealousy, she began to mistreat me. She told everyone we worked with that I was living at her house, as well as many other bad things about me.

I'd had enough of people using and abusing me. I realized that I needed a place for myself, so I decided to get a loan for an apartment. I found one in a new building that had recently been constructed. No one had lived in it before, so it truly felt like it was all mine. Finally, I had a space of my own and could claim my independence.

I hadn't lived in my new apartment very long when my boyfriend and I decided to take our relationship to the next level. He was kind and helpful, and he soon moved in with me. This man was the man who would become my first husband. I also became pregnant with my first daughter during this relationship.

My husband took good care of me and taught me things I needed to know, like how to drive. We had a good relationship with one another, but my mother-in-law didn't approve of us being together. She did not like me because she was angry that her son's money was going to me and our household and not to her. She wasn't content with simply making her disapproval known. She wanted revenge, and she took it in a very personal way.

Before my husband and I married, my mother-in-law went behind our backs and paid the pastor who was going to perform our ceremony to withhold our marriage license. When we found out, we simply got a new marriage license and didn't tell my mother-in-law. But every time she saw us after that, she would taunt me, saying that I wasn't really married to her son. She also tried to lie to my husband, but he didn't fall for her lies.

After a while, my husband got a new job and we moved our family to Fort Lauderdale. I loved the change. I finally started going back to school and got my certificate in home care. I also became a medical assistant while we were living there. I was finally beginning to feel like my life was getting back on track.

However, a new obstacle arose in one of the parts of my life that was most important to me: my marriage. I hadn't healed from my past sexual trauma, and my aversion to sex began to affect my relationship with my husband. He wanted something that I didn't always feel I could give to him.

My husband began to change as a person. He started abusing alcohol and drugs and would go to strip clubs after work with his coworkers. He also started to become angrier and more demanding. He would ask me to do sexual things that I wasn't comfortable doing and would become furious when I would refuse to do them. One night, while he was high, he asked me to do something that I wasn't comfortable with and I said no. He flew into a rage and threatened me with a knife. After that, he forced me to have sex with him.

Even though my husband had changed, I was determined to make our marriage work. I wanted to honor God and the promise I had made to my husband. But when I found out my husband was cheating on me, everything changed. A cousin of mine accompanied my husband one day when he went to town to cash a check without me. While they were in the car together, my husband asked my cousin for sex. She didn't do anything with him but she told me about what had happened. I was heartbroken and angry. I felt it was wrong of my cousin to go with my husband without me there but knew my husband held responsibility for asking her something like that. That became the breaking point in our relationship.

I began to rearrange my life so that I could leave my husband. I didn't want to be with someone who couldn't honor me, so I started looking for a new car and a new job. By that time, my husband was regularly violent with me, so I wanted a job that would allow me to live in a different place. I bought a Toyota and made the difficult decision to leave my daughter with my husband so I could find a new job.

I moved to Miramar to take a nannying and housekeeping position with a lawyer. I cared for her two children, cooked their meals, and cleaned the house for her. I stayed at the house during the week but on the weekends I had to find somewhere else to stay. A friend of mine lived in the area with her boyfriend and his friend who were both Haitian. She invited me to stay with them on the weekends and I accepted.

After a while, I decided to move back in with my husband. My job wasn't going well, and I wanted to try to repair our marriage. I didn't want my daughter to grow up in a broken home. While I was working in Miramar, my husband had told me that he was going to send our daughter to live with his mother. I was all right with that, but when I returned I discovered that he had actually sent her to live with a woman he was cheating on me with. Again, I was heartbroken. I had thought I could at least trust my husband with our daughter but he couldn't even fulfill that responsibility in our relationship. That lie was the final breaking point in our marriage.

I returned to my friend's home in Miramar and slept with my friend's roommate as revenge on my husband. I was so hurt and broken by what had happened that I only wanted to do something that could hurt him back. I told my friend's roommate that I wanted to get pregnant but he told me he didn't want to have a child because he didn't want to pay for child support. I told him that he wouldn't have to worry about that. I became pregnant with my fourth and youngest child by my friend's roommate. Even though he hadn't wanted a child, he was happy. He told me that he was going to move to Orlando and that he wanted me and my children to move with him so we could start our own life together. We moved into a beautiful house in Orlando, and my youngest child, my second daughter, was born early the next year.

Again, life seemed good. My new partner bought me a new car and helped me find an elder care job. He took a job as a carpenter. But I discovered that my partner had hidden something from me, something that contradicted my faith and how I wanted to live my life.

My partner was involved in witchcraft. It was something that he regularly practiced. I understood that it was part of how he had been raised, but I told him that he needed to stop so that we could properly care for our children and live for God. But he didn't stop. No matter what I said, he kept practicing witchcraft—and it began to threaten our family.

One day, one of my daughters touched a ritualistic object that belonged to my partner. When he found out, he said that something bad would happen to her because he was the only person who was supposed to touch that object. Later that day, my daughter fell and cut her face.

HE SAW THE BEST IN ME

My partner and I were together for seven years but as our relationship progressed it fell apart due to the lack of communication and my partner's continued involvement with witchcraft. Our relationship really began to come undone when I found out that the house we were living in, the house that I thought belonged to my partner, was actually owned by his brother. I was shocked. I had been paying for the mortgage, but the money was going somewhere else and I didn't know where that was. My partner's brother had been making the payments on the house. When he showed up and demanded that we leave, there was nothing that we could do. He evicted us and we had to move into an apartment.

While we were living in the apartment, I didn't work for a while. My partner was the only one working and he would go to the park to play football after work to let off steam. One night, I asked to use his phone while he was in the shower. As I was using his phone, he received a text message from a girl. I opened it and found out that my partner was cheating on me. The girl's message said that she enjoyed the day at the park with him. I took down her number, and the next day when my partner was at work, I called her. When she answered the phone, I told her who I was. She replied that she knew about me and began to say terrible things to me. She told me that my partner said I was lazy because I wasn't working, that he had to pay all the bills, and that he didn't need me. He wanted a working girl. I ended the call and that night I confronted him.

He denied everything she said and told me that the girl had been lying, but I knew that she was telling me the truth. I lost my trust in him, and we began to drift apart. We still lived together, and I still cooked and cleaned for him, but we didn't talk. We didn't have sex. We just existed around one another. I met someone else and dated him for a while, but it turned out he was lying to me about his name and his marital status. I went back to my old partner, but our relationship didn't improve.

In 2010, my divorce from my first husband was made official. I also applied for citizenship and found a new job. I started to make good money and soon I was in the position to leave my partner. My partner didn't want me to leave. He was angry and threatened to kill me with witchcraft. I told him that if he tried to do anything to me, God would protect me. I took my two daughters and left. Even though our relationship had gone on for so long and his witchcraft used to frighten me, I felt strengthened by my faith. I believed God would protect me and my family and guide me to a better path.

I didn't hear from my ex-partner for several days after I left. Eventually, I learned that he'd had a stroke shortly after I left him and was in the hospital. The staff had been neglecting him, so I took care of him when I visited him. The doctors told me that his stroke had been so severe that he wasn't expected to recover his speech or his ability to walk. I could feel God telling me that I should look after my ex-partner, so when he was discharged, I took him in.

My ex-partner's path to recovery was a slow one, but as time went on, he recovered his abilities to speak and walk. Free to pursue my own path, I finally turned my attention toward myself, my family, and following God's guidance.

5

NEW BLESSINGS AND BEGINNINGS

As I turned my focus to changing my life, I worked hard to improve in my job. My educational background had done a lot to hinder my career, but I had something that helped me overcome that. My work ethic and attention to detail always made me stand out, and my commitment to being a hardworking employee paid off. I was promoted twice at my job within two months.

Since I didn't rely on my daughters' fathers for any financial or parental help, these promotions came at a time when I really needed them. My daughters were in school and depended on me to be their rock. I didn't want to let them down, so I worked hard. Although my hard work paid off financially, I soon found that I had to make sacrifices in other ways.

Because I was working so hard, I often had to stay late at work, which meant I wasn't always able to pick up my daughters from school. I always tried my best to make it on time but I was late more often than not. This continued for some time until the school administration contacted me about picking my daughters up late. They said that if I continued to pick up my daughters late, they would have to involve the Department of Children and Families. I explained my situation to the school administrator. I told her that my daughters had no one else but me and that I was working as hard as I could to build a good life for them. To my surprise, she took compassion on me and said she would help me. She began to wait with my children after school, essentially providing me with free childcare. She would tell me, "Take all the time you need." Perhaps it was a small thing to her but to me it was a blessing sent straight from heaven. I knew God was watching out for me and my family.

Even though my life was slowly improving in many ways, I still felt that something was missing. I began to pray to God for a partner. Even though I was capable of caring for my children on my own, I wanted someone to help me, someone who would walk alongside me throughout my life. I also wanted someone who was educated, but also understood what it was like to live in poverty. I'd already been married three times by that point. Besides my first husband, I had married two men from Jamaica. The first one had tried to manipulate me into using the money I was saving to bring my eldest son to the United States for him, proving he wasn't father material. The other was simply using me so he could come to the United States to be with a woman he was in a relationship with, a relationship that he had kept hidden from me. I was tired of the lies and the emotional strain. I wanted someone I knew I could count on. More importantly, I wanted someone who loved and honored God.

In 2013, my life suffered another blow. My landlord at the time began making romantic advances toward me. I knew he was married, and still held by my commitment to never be in a relationship with a married man. I'd come so far and I didn't want that kind of trouble in my life again. Around the same time, my boss asked me to demote myself at work. He said he would pay me more if I did. I was afraid of being unable to support my children and felt like I couldn't say no to him. So I demoted myself.

Little did I know that it was all part of a scheme to make me leave the company. Of course, my boss didn't start paying me more after I accepted my demotion. When I found out that extra money was actually being taken out of my paycheck, my company's HR department did nothing to help me. I hired a lawyer, but I lost the case. I lost my job and my house. My landlord had been threatening to take me to court because I was having trouble making my rent payments and because he wanted revenge on me for refusing to date him. Fortunately, because of his conduct toward me, he didn't act on his threats. He was afraid of his wife finding out what happened. So he settled for evicting me.

A woman from my church was kind enough to open her home to me and my children. Again, I felt grateful and blessed; I knew God was still watching over me and I trusted Him to take care of me and my family. But despite this woman's generosity, our lives were still hard. We were crammed together in a small space and my eldest daughter was struggling with bedwetting, something I was trying to help her deal with.

My situation reinforced my desire to find a loving, godly partner and I didn't give up hope that God would bring the right person into my life at the right time. Sure enough, one night in October 2013, God told me in a dream, "Woman of God, your husband is coming in one month." That same month, my church held an event on Halloween night, which I took part in. I went dressed as Cleopatra and sang in the church choir. As I was singing, I could feel someone watching me. I looked out into the congregation and I saw him: the man God had shown me in my dream.

His name was Thakur Sukhdeo. He came to church again the next night and I sang in the choir again. The whole time I was singing, we couldn't take our eyes off each other. After the service was over, I approached Thakur and asked him, "Are you my husband?"

He was surprised by my question, and when I asked him for his phone number, he gave me an incorrect number. I got his real number from a friend and we soon started talking. I learned that he had been in prison for seven years because of illegal possession of a gun. I also learned that he was a kind and compassionate man. Eventually, I told Thakur about my living situation and he invited me and my children to move in with him and his family. He said there would be enough room for all of us.

Life with Thakur was so different from everything else I had ever experienced. He would play the same gospel song for me every night, and we talked a great deal. He also respected my boundaries and wishes in a way that no other man ever had. We waited until my divorce from my third husband was finalized to start a serious relationship, and Thakur was completely understanding during the waiting period.

When we got married, we didn't plan an elaborate ceremony. We simply went to get our marriage license, had a private ceremony at our church, and then went out for lunch after. We were married on February 27, 2014. Every day since then, Thakur has lived up to the vision God showed me. He is a respectful, loving husband and I am so thankful to have him in my life.

Today, all of my children live in the United States. My eldest son is in the army, attending college, and engaged to a lovely young woman. My second eldest just turned twenty-one. My two daughters are both in school and live with me and my husband; my youngest daughter attends IB classes. I am so proud of all of them and so grateful to God that my family is whole again. My children are doing amazing things with their lives and I am excited to see where they will go as they grow older.

As for me, I am finally living the life I wanted, the same life that I feel God has called me to live. My husband and I have an outreach ministry together. We reach out to people in our community who need help and guidance. Years ago, I couldn't understand why so many hurting and hurtful people kept coming into my life. For a while, the presence of such people in my life made me feel as if I were somehow being held back from what God wanted me to do. Then I realized something: I am connected to broken people because God is calling me to help them. My ministry is a broken ministry,

HE SAW THE BEST IN ME

and I am grateful that I am able to help others find healing from brokenness. God saw the best in me, after all. He blessed me with a loving family, healing, and inner strength. I believe that He sees the best in others too and can help them find healing from brokenness.

6

GOD CAN TAKE ANYBODY FROM LOW TO HIGH

I had a few different reasons for wanting to write this book and share my story with others, but one of the main reasons is that I want other people to know that no matter how terrible life might get, there is always hope for them. You are never so far gone or so broken that God will not want you back or be unable to save you. I suffered sexual abuse, molestation, physical abuse, and more throughout my life, but God gave me strength. The things that happened to me never destroyed my spirit because of my faith in God. I knew that He was calling me to live for greater things and I was, and still am, confident that He will help me fulfill that calling.

I want you to know that you are capable of overcoming whatever has happened to you in your life through God's love and healing. Anything or anyone that has hurt you in your life is not more powerful than God. He will always love you, no matter what you do. According to Psalm 139, there is no height to which we can ascend or any depths we can plummet to that will keep us from God. His love is always around us, even in the moments we feel most alone and forgotten. And that love is always accessible to us. All we have to do is accept it.

I understand that life can be scary, especially if you're young and all you've ever known is pain. I hope that you will take comfort in God's message of love and hope. I hope that you never give up fighting for a better life and that you never settle for a life that doesn't fit you. My prayer is that you, reading this right now, will keep pursuing God's calling and goodness in this life. It is there and you are capable of finding it. Always remember: God can take anybody from low to high. I'm now happily married with four wonderful children. My husband and I are Evangelists with our ministry, Restore the Broken by Faith Evangelistic International ministry. We help with mission feeding the homeless and reaching out to the less fortunate.

StoryTerrace

www.ingramcontent.com/pod-product-compliance
Lightning Source LLC
Chambersburg PA
CBHW061031180426
43194CB00036B/168